CHOSEN

&

UNFROZEN

An inspirational testimony of why to never give up on your purposed fulfilled dreams and visions!

by:

Dr. Martin Alan Bryant

- CEO of: Aged Not

THANK YOU, FIRST AND FOREMOST TO: MY FIRST LOVE, THE ONE I'M ABSOLUTELY IN LOVE WITH! MY CREATOR, MY KING, MY RULER, MY HEAVENLY FATHER, MY DELIVERER, MY TEACHER, MY BEST FRIEND NOT OF THIS WORLD, MY COMFORTER, MY COUNSELOR, MY COACH, MY PERSONAL TRAINER, MY MASTER, MY EVERYTHING!

LOVE AND SHOUT OUTS TO MY FAM:

My Wife 4 Life

Moms, Bio-Bro, My 3 Sisters, Nephews, Nieces, Cousins

My Seeds: B-bop, Re-bop, Bop-Bop, Bizzy-bop, Dainty-bop

All In-laws, All my brothers & sisters in The Messiah

Darcy, Lavenia, Craig, Dre, Sharon, Ke-Ke, (thanks 4 Prayers!)

The Aged Not Caged Team/Fam:

Paree Kidd-Curtis Wesley-Curteca Davis-Dominic Wesley

My passed on Fam-Daddy, Dell Sr, Lamont, Jerry, Mama Rice

Last and surely not least to the haters, to the **Foes**, right under my **Nose**! I love Ya'll and thank ya'll! I would not be in the place I'm at without ya'll! You know who you are, so I don't need to **Name you** or **Blame you**! – SHALAWAM [PEACE BE UNTO YOU]

GENESIS 50:15-21

[15] And when Joseph's brethren saw that their father was dead, they said, Joseph will peradventure hate us, and will certainly requite us all the evil which we did unto him.

[16] And they sent a messenger unto Joseph, saying, Thy father did command before he died, saying,

[17] So shall ye say unto Joseph, Forgive, I pray thee now, the trespass of thy brethren, and their sin; for they did unto thee evil: and now, we pray thee, forgive the trespass of the servants of the God of thy father. And Joseph wept when they spake unto him.

[18] And his brethren also went and fell down before his face; and they said, Behold, we be thy servants.

[19] And Joseph said unto them, Fear not: for am I in the place of God?

[20] But as for you, ye thought evil against me; but God meant it unto good, to bring to pass, as it is this day, to save much people alive.

[21] Now therefore fear ye not: I will nourish you, and your little ones. And he comforted them, and spake kindly unto them.

LitPrime Solutions
21250 Hawthorne Blvd
Suite 500, Torrance, CA 90503
www.litprime.com
Phone: 1-800-981-9893

Published by LitPrime Solutions: 04/25/2024

ISBN: 979-8-88703-350-1(sc)
ISBN: 979-8-88703-351-8(e)

Library of Congress Control Number: 2024904668

LIST OF CHAPTERS:

PRELUDE:

The year is 2023, the day is Thursday November 23, that is referred to as *Thanksgiving Day* in North America where I was born and raised. I have just turned 54 years of age 21 days prior to this day, and I'm grateful to be another age, to have been blessed with another day, another year, etc., etc.

I have been invited to three different Thanksgiving gatherings, with family and like family, and I'm told how good I look, and I'm being flirted with, and as usual it's not going to my head, especially this year.....why?

Behind the smile, {smiles can cover up a lot sometimes} I'm thankful, grateful, and Blessed........however in the back of my mind, I'm lonely as heck! I miss my wife whom has placed a fraudulent protection order against me and had me removed from the home we share, I'm not able to see my 3 children, except for when I visit their schools, my wife of 16 years has said she wants a separation, and it's for no good reason at all to me...., my adult son,[20] whom I have raised for 16 years, never once referring to him as my step son, told me that I'm not his daddy after cussing me out, while he's residing in the home, I said he could come back home to, and his friend down the street from the home, I have been put out of, has moved in to that same home, and this 18 year old kid (huge though, about 6'5" 275 lbs.) assaulted me physically in front of my 3 other kids and in front of one of my sisters and niece to my shame. (He admitted that he, knew that I really did not want to fight with him, because I still saw him as a kid, and in my time, a teenager would never dare call out, or attack his friends daddy! In my days as a youth, we feared our friends, and neighbors daddies!)

I'm working back at the job I had left, 4 years prior, to pursue a potential 6 figure income. (You always will have my gratitude, P.K. for you pulling the necessary strings so I could, at least have a steady job). Here I am currently a Preacher of The Gospel, a holder of an earned Doctorate degree in Business Administration, and a licensed Life, Health, and Medical insurance Broker, A CEO of an LLC, A self-employed 5-star Uber driver and now I'm driving a transportation bus, [$20 per hour] and living back with family in the same home I was raised in since, I was 8 years old...[*I must notate, that I was grateful for a bed, & shelter*] It felt like a nightmare.........., however as you will realize as I came to realize (through Divine interventions, revelations, and conformations, all in this book) that to live your dreams you have to endure nightmares first! The majority are taught and believe just the opposite, they will do anything and everything to live their dreams, not realizing that in doing so, they will 'FOREVER' live *out*, and live *in* their nightmares...

MATTHEW 16:25-26

25 For whosoever will save his life shall lose it: and whosoever will lose his life for my sake shall find it.

26 For what is a man profited, if he shall gain the whole world, and lose his own soul? or what shall a man give in exchange for his soul?

CHAPTER ONE (1)
FROM MY **BIRTH**, TO MY **WORTH**
[JEREMIAH 1:1-8]

1 The words of Jeremiah the son of Hilkiah, of the priests that were in Anathoth in the land of Benjamin:

2 To whom the word of the LORD came in the days of Josiah the son of Amon king of Judah, in the thirteenth year of his reign.

3 It came also in the days of Jehoiakim the son of Josiah king of Judah, unto the end of the eleventh year of Zedekiah the son of Josiah king of Judah, unto the carrying away of Jerusalem captive in the fifth month.

4 Then the word of the LORD came unto me, saying,

5 Before I formed thee in the belly I knew thee; and before thou camest forth out of the womb I sanctified thee, and I ordained thee a prophet unto the nations.

6 Then said I, Ah, Lord GOD! behold, I cannot speak: for I am a child.

7 But the LORD said unto me, Say not, I am a child: for thou shalt go to all that I shall send thee, and whatsoever I command thee thou shalt speak.

8 Be not afraid of their faces: for I am with thee to deliver thee, saith the LORD.

As I had mentioned in the prelude, as this book is published in the year of 2024 CE, I'm 54 years of age, which to some will be viewed as aged, to some middle-aged, or to some as young. I don't care how I'm viewed age wise or any other wise, I'm thankful to be blessed, to where I don't have to take no medications for my physical well-being or mental well-being. I'm a spirit-filled man, full of all the fruit of the spirit, and greatfully......
I DON'T HAVE TO **SMOKE**, TO TELL A **JOKE**!
I DON'T HAVE TO **DRINK**, TO CLEARLY **THINK**!

I don't mean either one of those, to make it seem as if, I'm saying that I'm holier than thou, no! It was not always this way for me, you see......
I'm the youngest of 5 siblings from my mother's womb, my only biological brother and I are 8 years apart, and although there is no such thing as a mistake with a child being born, I have been told that my mother had difficulty carrying me in her womb, (her last child, she carried in her womb) and I have prophetic understanding of this now, that it's because, the devil, did not want me to make it, ...why you ask? The devil knew that I was a chosen vessel before I even exited my mother's womb!

I was born on a Sunday, [First day of The week] and as I have been told, a police department rushed and escorted my mother to the hospital for me to be delivered. [I was born on an Air Force base right outside of the city, that I was raised in which is Kansas City, Missouri, my daddy was not present because he was currently in The USAF away on active duty]. The interesting thing about it was that the police force from the small town, where I was born, is the same police department that came after me 30 years later, resulting in my spiritual rebirth!

As I grew up, even in my toddler years my most recent memories are when I was 3 years old. At the tender age of 3 years old, I started to experience seeing things which would be considered unusual to other people, even kids.

For example the same house that I was born and raised in, when I was 3 years old, I remember walking past our floor model television in the front room. I had taken three steps past the television on a rainy evening, and I remember being lead to turn my head and look at the television that I had just passed, and as I looked back, a yellow, jagged bolt of lightning, came through the closed window (without any damage to the glass) and literally pushed the television knob in, and the television cut off! I lie not! I remember seeing the knob (a black pull out, push in knob that was about an inch long) pushed in, and I heard the click sound it made whenever I remember the knob was pushed in or pulled out.

I immediately ran and told my family what I saw and what had happened, and my daddy being the strong man of the house that he was, came and pulled the knob out on the television and it came back on. My daddy never said he didn't believe me out right, he just said that what I saw was hard to believe and who could blame him! I know what I saw way back then, and as ridiculous as it sounds, I know what I saw!

About 5 years later at the age of eight, (same house I'm in right now, writing this book) is when I started experiencing demonic attacks. In all seriousness I lie not. I became a bed-wetter, because I would be held down by unseen forces as I would be awakened out of a deep sleep. I would have nightmares of "shadows" running towards me, and wake up screaming, only to be held down by forces I could not see. I would also be scared to go to sleep, and as my mother lovingly would try to make me go to sleep, I would hear my sisters laughing at me through the bedroom walls.

(I forgave Ya'll though, even back then!)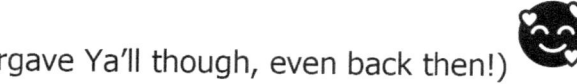

Also at this time in my 8 years of life, it became noticeable that I was very set-apart from all the rest of my family. My family were all fit, I was chubby. My family, siblings and parents, had black hair, I was born with red hair, which later turned sandy brown. My family was all nice looking, and according to my daddy, I looked like a little alien!

Daddy was right, because I did, because I was!

Now this part here, was no laughing matter, back then!

This is when the bullying started! Most kids face a bully, or have to deal with bullying at some point in their lives, so I'm not trying to single myself out, or minimize my situation or someone else's situation. From pre-school until now, I've faced bullying and it doesn't feel good at the time; however HALLELUYAH ***I know now what it brings about!*** It's no coincidence that one of the services our business offers is "Pulley The Bully". Bullying never feels good at the moment; however it will bring you way up in life later, so that you can help others. **Bully**=Seek to harm, intimidate, or coerce someone seen as vulnerable. As my sister in The Messiah (What's up Big Sis!) once told me years ago, after a church service......Martin..
You were picked out, to be picked on!
Prophetess you were right on point!

Why they would come to bully me	Why I was being bullied	How I was being bullied	Purpose for me being bullied
Cause I was a fat kid	They were jealous of my big frame, to be a young kid	Other kids would laugh at me being a kid with a pot belly	To come out from among them. **II Corinthians 6:14-18**
Always talking about my mama	They were jealous, of my mama's unique look	They would say my mama looked like a gypsy.	To come out from among them. **II Corinthians 6:14-18**
Making fun of my brown hair	They were jealous of my unique appearance	Constantly accused of never combing or washing my hair	To come out from among them. **II Corinthians 6:14-18**
They said I was a scrubby athlete	They were jealous of what I could do, despite my weight	Would never let me play any type of sports with them	To come out from among them. **II Corinthians 6:14-18**

What they come to bully me about	Why I'm being bullied	How they attempt to bully me	What this bullying shows me is....
They say I dress to flamboyant	They would dress flamboyant also, but are too worried about what others would think about them!	They try to get me, to perceive myself as something that I'm not, and make it like GOD is saying that I need to change how I dress	I'm Blessed! **Matthew 5:10-12**
You don't know what you're talking about when you preach or teach	They want to preach and teach The TRUTH; however they are too scared to go against what they have been traditionally taught!	Their have been and there are several men and women out there today, that talk and plot about ways they desire to ex-communicate me!	I'm Blessed! **Matthew 5:10-12**
We believe you are only doing this for fame and fortune	They can see that my heart is really for the Messiah and what he has for me to do! They realize this, and it convicts them, because they are all about just the fame and fortune!	Spreading rumors, trying to figure out my net worth, and how much is coming into the business, where I'm living, and how I'm providing for my family, what I'm driving etc.	I'm Blessed! **Matthew 5:10-12**
A real Man of GOD would not shave his head, and work-out, and be mindful of his diet!	When people are unhappy with themselves, they will throw stones at you, because you being happy, with self, and your place in The Messiah most importantly, is a direct exposure of their, unhappiness, slothfulness, bitterness and uncleanness!	I hear from BHI camps often that I should let what little hair I can grow, grow out on my head! (although I have never seen any of them looking like George Jefferson with the ball spot yet! None ever have invested in getting me a hair transplant either!)	I'm Blessed! **Matthew 5:10-12**

Back when I was a youth, constant bullying lead me unawares into a dangerous place of me having low self esteem about myself, into which I started attempting to drown my sorrows in alcohol and sexual relationships with older women, that accepted me as I was, being different, but having a physique that they admired. I did grab ahold to a positive throughout being bullied, and that was that I wanted to look like the superheroes in Marvel comic books (which I'm not ashamed to say, I still collect today, and will pass them on to my kids one day) so, I started working out at 16 years old and achieved that goal! The only challenge was me having difficulty adjusting to all the attention I started to get from going from fat to fit! As I had mentioned also a paragraph ago, as a teenager into a young adult, females my age were not feeling me; however older women from 40 to 50, gladly accepted me as their boy-toy! I'm not bragging and this is nothing to brag about…..I was not a Man of The MOST HIGH I was surely running from The Chosen destiny on my life as a pre-destined Chosen vessel, and I was exhausted most of the time, because a man, young man, etc.'s body is not to be used by women as their play thing! During my early 20's the devil had his hooks all into me, deep! I praise and thank The MOST HIGH that, I was not killed by a jealous boyfriend, or a hater period, because believe you me, I had haters, up close and personal, and haters at a distance that hated on me because of my lifestyle, and macho swagger at this time. I was a womanizer to the fullest extent…..and if I had died in that mess, I would have went to a place of eternal torment, with never an exit sign in sight!

The following is a true story, that I will tell as many times as often, to be used to inspire a Chosen Soul!

In 1997 at the age of 27 years old, I was in The Bahama islands with a girlfriend. We were at a tourist resort, and I went to go ask some people where the nearest bathroom was at. I approached a man and a woman and I asked if they could direct me to the nearest bathroom, the man took a look at me and said, "you look like you could be one of my relatives that lives on this island"! The man said that because of my light eyes, and complexion, it looked as if we could be related. I could sense that the man was sincere saying this, and I did see that we favored and I noticed that this man was very well built, and as he says follow me and I will show you where the nearest bathroom is, he noticed and comments that I had a nice physique, and that many men on the island were strong also. I continue to follow this well built melinated brother, then all of a sudden he stops in his tracks, turns to me and says….."You ever had trouble fitting in"? I astonishly said "Yes". Then he goes and tells me, "It's irritating being rejected often isn't it'? I reluctantly, but astonishly said "Yes". Then he said "Everything you try to do never works out the way you expect does it?" Instead of saying yes this time, I reached out to shake his hand while saying," Man that's a heck of a gift you got"! He did not shake my hand, and he rebuked me sharply by saying in a heavy Bohemian accent "It is not a gift, this is what GOD is showing me right now! We talked for about 15 minutes, and to highlight what he told me are these following things:

> ➢ Give your life to GOD, be in a relationship with HIM, don't become religious
> ➢ There are not many at all like Us, and that we are Chosen warriors of GOD
> ➢ I likened us to the warriors on the t.v. show highlander, not immortal of course
> ➢ GOD will always keep money in your wallet (he shows me his wallet is fat!)
> ➢ Your life will be challenging, but trust in GOD to bring you out
> ➢ The next time He and I would meet would be in Heaven!

After we finished talking, he said "ok I will let you go ahead and use the bathroom now", (The thing is, I went although I really didn't even have to go after hearing what he had to say! No lie!)

As I'm coming from the bathroom, my girlfriend walks up to me with tears in her eyes and says I was worried about you! I told her that I was okay, and what me and the man, talked about, and of course she thought I was crazy!

Ironically, after we get back in town, about 3 months later, I had a co-worker that was contemplating suicide, and I would talk to him, and tell him don't do it, just because I felt that was the right thing to do. The same co-worker would thank me and tell me, that I reminded him of a preacher, and he felt that was. one of the purposes on my life! I told the same girlfriend, what my co-worker had said, and lo and behold, she thought I was crazy again and accused me of believing everything that anyone and everyone would tell me! {Bless her heart, it wasn't her, it was the devil putting that on her mind, due to this being something he always feared, I would accept!}

It would be a full 3 years before, I accepted The Messiah and what he had Chosen for me to do, in his name and for his glory!

[ONE OF MANY THINGS I LEARNED IN LIFE, IS THAT WHEN YOU ARE AT YOUR WORST...THE CREATOR IS UP TO HIS BEST!]

All of this will be explained in the proceeding chapters of this book.

JOHN 15:16

[16] Ye have not chosen me, but I have chosen you, and ordained you, that ye should go and bring forth fruit, and that your fruit should remain: that whatsoever ye shall ask of the Father in my name, he may give it you.

CHAPTER TWO (2)
WHAT'S FOR **DESSERT**, NOTHING BUT CHURCH **HURT!**

LUKE 6:22-23

22 Blessed are ye, when men shall hate you, and when they shall separate you from their company, and shall reproach you, and cast out your name as evil, for the Son of man's sake.

23 Rejoice ye in that day, and leap for joy: for, behold, your reward is great in heaven: for in the like manner did their fathers unto the prophets.

Now let me set the record straight, I received and endured a lot of church hurt in the past, and I forgive and forgave all that came against me. One of many things that I have learned is that, chosen people are not traditional people, and traditional people want to keep their traditions, and you will be seen as a threat, if they feel you are a threat to their tradition(s)!

Not to justify anything or anyone, it's just that men and women have spent hours and big dollars, to enjoy a reputable, and a prestige life, and here comes the chosen to boldly let them know what their following is and doing is not the TRUTH!

Grand Example:

ACTS 22:1-20

22 Men, brethren, and fathers, hear ye my defence which I make now unto you.

2 (And when they heard that he spake in the Hebrew tongue to them, they kept the more silence: and he saith,)

3 I am verily a man which am a Jew, born in Tarsus, a city in Cilicia, yet brought up in this city at the feet of Gamaliel, and taught according to the perfect manner of the law of the fathers, and was zealous toward God, as ye all are this day.

4 And I persecuted this way unto the death, binding and delivering into prisons both men and women.

5 As also the high priest doth bear me witness, and all the estate of the elders: from whom also I received letters unto the brethren, and went to Damascus, to bring them which were there bound unto Jerusalem, for to be punished.

⁶ And it came to pass, that, as I made my journey, and was come nigh unto Damascus about noon, suddenly there shone from heaven a great light round about me.

⁷ And I fell unto the ground, and heard a voice saying unto me, Saul, Saul, why persecutest thou me?

⁸ And I answered, Who art thou, Lord? And he said unto me, I am Jesus of Nazareth, whom thou persecutest.

⁹ And they that were with me saw indeed the light, and were afraid; but they heard not the voice of him that spake to me.

¹⁰ And I said, What shall I do, LORD? And the Lord said unto me, Arise, and go into Damascus; and there it shall be told thee of all things which are appointed for thee to do.

¹¹ And when I could not see for the glory of that light, being led by the hand of them that were with me, I came into Damascus.

¹² And one Ananias, a devout man according to the law, having a good report of all the Jews which dwelt there,

¹³ Came unto me, and stood, and said unto me, Brother Saul, receive thy sight. And the same hour I looked up upon him.

¹⁴ And he said, The God of our fathers hath chosen thee, that thou shouldest know his will, and see that Just One, and shouldest hear the voice of his mouth.

¹⁵ For thou shalt be his witness unto all men of what thou hast seen and heard.

¹⁶ And now why tarriest thou? arise, and be baptized, and wash away thy sins, calling on the name of the Lord.

¹⁷ And it came to pass, that, when I was come again to Jerusalem, even while I prayed in the temple, I was in a trance;

¹⁸ And saw him saying unto me, Make haste, and get thee quickly out of Jerusalem: for they will not receive thy testimony concerning me.

¹⁹ And I said, Lord, they know that I imprisoned and beat in every synagogue them that believed on thee:

²⁰ And when the blood of thy martyr Stephen was shed, I also was standing by, and consenting unto his death, and kept the raiment of them that slew him.

Followers of The way, (as they were called, not Christians) were a threat to Saul, and being a religious man of prestige, felt that he had to eliminate this threat to his belief, that he was fanatical about!

Another example non-Biblical:

The majority of people want things easier, but not different. The majority of people get too comfortable with the same old, same old, and will resist, reject, and take offense to anyone that offers a fresh, and a better way of doing things.

Biblical example:

ACTS 18:1-6

After these things Paul departed from Athens, and came to Corinth;

2 And found a certain Jew named Aquila, born in Pontus, lately come from Italy, with his wife Priscilla; (because that Claudius had commanded all Jews to depart from Rome:) and came unto them.

3 And because he was of the same craft, he abode with them, and wrought: for by their occupation they were tentmakers.

4 And he reasoned in the synagogue every sabbath, and persuaded the Jews and the Greeks.

5 And when Silas and Timotheus were come from Macedonia, Paul was pressed in the spirit, and testified to the Jews that Jesus was Christ.

6 And when they opposed themselves, and blasphemed, he shook his raiment, and said unto them, Your blood be upon your own heads; I am clean; from henceforth I will go unto the Gentiles.

There will always be those you can persuade and those that you cannot persuade!

The chosen are not sent out to reach everybody, they are sent out to reach somebody, out of everybody! If the chosen expect to reach everybody, they are in for an eye opening disappointment!

I never stepped into a church building thinking I was better than anybody, but let me tell you, those elders and those that had been in church (the building) longer than me, sure thought they was better! Through all that abuse, {psychological} and all of that rejection, betrayal, and embarrassment, I never was ran out of the building, nor did I stop praising my CREATOR! I was off milk and ready to eat meat and all I was served was …..Dessert in the form of church Hurt!

MATTHEW 20:1-16

For the kingdom of heaven is like unto a man that is an householder, which went out early in the morning to hire labourers into his vineyard.

[2] And when he had agreed with the labourers for a penny a day, he sent them into his vineyard.

[3] And he went out about the third hour, and saw others standing idle in the marketplace,

[4] And said unto them; Go ye also into the vineyard, and whatsoever is right I will give you. And they went their way.

[5] Again he went out about the sixth and ninth hour, and did likewise.

[6] And about the eleventh hour he went out, and found others standing idle, and saith unto them, Why stand ye here all the day idle?

[7] They say unto him, Because no man hath hired us. He saith unto them, Go ye also into the vineyard; and whatsoever is right, that shall ye receive.

[8] So when even was come, the lord of the vineyard saith unto his steward, Call the labourers, and give them their hire, beginning from the last unto the first.

[9] And when they came that were hired about the eleventh hour, they received every man a penny.

[10] But when the first came, they supposed that they should have received more; and they likewise received every man a penny.

[11] And when they had received it, they murmured against the goodman of the house,

[12] Saying, These last have wrought but one hour, and thou hast made them equal unto us, which have borne the burden and heat of the day.

[13] But he answered one of them, and said, Friend, I do thee no wrong: didst not thou agree with me for a penny?

[14] Take that thine is, and go thy way: I will give unto this last, even as unto thee.

[15] Is it not lawful for me to do what I will with mine own? Is thine eye evil, because I am good?

[16] So the last shall be first, and the first last: for many be called, but few chosen.

The called have a problem with the chosen, and they have a problem with the "chooser" of the chosen! I submitted to The Messiah in the year 2000, after all those years of running from my purpose, and 3 years later, I was preaching boldly, 10 toes down! The called had a problem with that, just like the example of Matthew 20, above! Something else the chosen need to beware of:

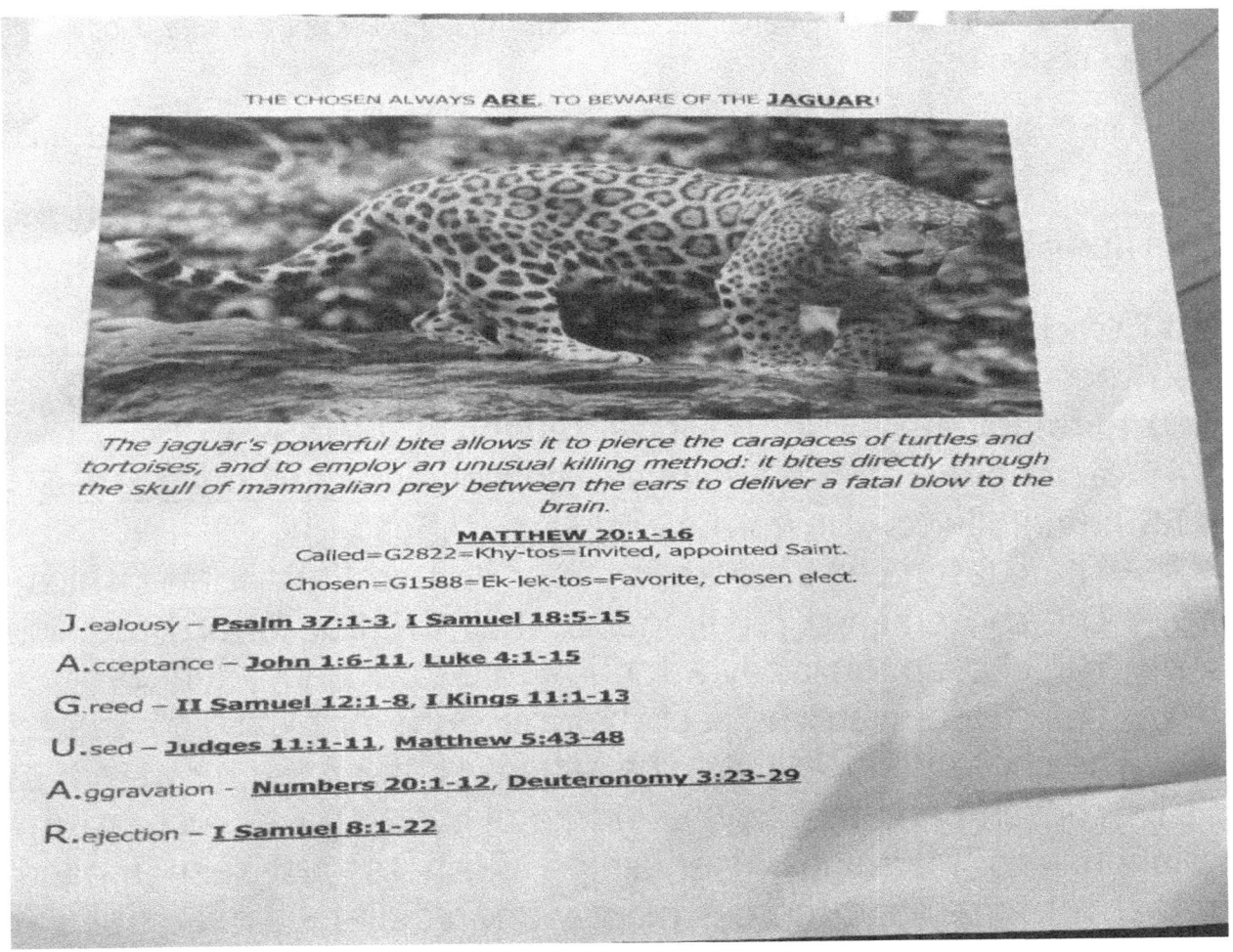

THE CHOSEN ALWAYS **ARE**, TO BEWARE OF THE **JAGUAR**!

The jaguar's powerful bite allows it to pierce the carapaces of turtles and tortoises, and to employ an unusual killing method: it bites directly through the skull of mammalian prey between the ears to deliver a fatal blow to the brain.

MATTHEW 20:1-16
Called=G2822=Khy-tos=Invited, appointed Saint.
Chosen=G1588=Ek-lek-tos=Favorite, chosen elect.

J.ealousy – **Psalm 37:1-3, I Samuel 18:5-15**

A.cceptance – **John 1:6-11, Luke 4:1-15**

G.reed – **II Samuel 12:1-8, I Kings 11:1-13**

U.sed – **Judges 11:1-11, Matthew 5:43-48**

A.ggravation - **Numbers 20:1-12, Deuteronomy 3:23-29**

R.ejection – **I Samuel 8:1-22**

One of many lessons, I have taught in the month of January 2024 on the chosen, and the predators that stalk and seek to attack them! I learned a lot about The Jaguar! Human beings are mammals, and this is talking about an unclean Jaguar spirit! The unclean spirit {demon} tries to deliver the fatal bite, to destroy your mind!{soul} I didn't realize until being given this, how many Jaguars I encountered in Church! Last but surely not least, The Church is within us, we are The Church and are therefore allowed to assembly where directed, and that doesn't mean in a building!

ACTS 16:13
13 And on the sabbath we went out of the city by a river side, where prayer was wont to be made; and we sat down, and spake unto the women which resorted thither.
[The Apostle Paul did it the right way, on the right day!]

CHAPTER THREE (3)
T.R.I.P.S. OF THE CHOSEN IN **RELATIONSHIPS**

I CORINTHIANS 7:10-11

[10] And unto the married I command, yet not I, but the Lord, Let not the wife depart from her husband:

[11] But and if she depart, let her remain unmarried or be reconciled to her husband: and let not the husband put away his wife.

Trips=To catch a foot onto something and stumble and fall.

#1T.oxicity=quality of being very harmful. **I Corinthians 15:33**
#2R.ebellioness=open resistance to a ruler. **I Samuel 15:23**
#3I.nattentiveness=Not paying attention. **I John 4:1**
#4P.assionate=Intense feelings of sexual love. **Judges 16:4-6**
#5S.hamefullness=Unworthiness. **Luke 15:11-32**
#1 – The chosen can't let other's in or around their relationships
#2 – The chosen can't rebel against their Creator for any reason
#3 – The chosen must pay attention to details and red flags
#4 – The chosen can't neglect their mission, for pleasure's sake
#5- The chosen should never be ashamed of a fresh new start
The chosen need to follow all of the above to have successful relationships,[Marriages, Friendships, Business] just keep in mind that with marriage there is more work required. I'm a strong proponent against divorce, and although there are outs for certain circumstances, if at least one person in a married couple is a believer, it can be worked out! Prayer is a powerful weapon in The believer's hand's and of course there is no problem, including in marriage for The Creator to fix! Let separation occur for a reason and for a season, and then reconcile, once The Creator lets it be known that it's reconciliation time! I'm currently practicing what I'm preaching! [*Daily battle for relationships!*]

In a marriage that is ordained by THE MOST HIGH there should never be any reason for divorce!

THE MOST HIGH put two individuals together until death does them part!

GENESIS 29:1-35

29 Then Jacob went on his journey, and came into the land of the people of the east.

2 And he looked, and behold a well in the field, and, lo, there were three flocks of sheep lying by it; for out of that well they watered the flocks: and a great stone was upon the well's mouth.

3 And thither were all the flocks gathered: and they rolled the stone from the well's mouth, and watered the sheep, and put the stone again upon the well's mouth in his place.

4 And Jacob said unto them, My brethren, whence be ye? And they said, Of Haran are we.

5 And he said unto them, Know ye Laban the son of Nahor? And they said, We know him.

6 And he said unto them, Is he well? And they said, He is well: and, behold, Rachel his daughter cometh with the sheep.

7 And he said, Lo, it is yet high day, neither is it time that the cattle should be gathered together: water ye the sheep, and go and feed them.

8 And they said, We cannot, until all the flocks be gathered together, and till they roll the stone from the well's mouth; then we water the sheep.

9 And while he yet spake with them, Rachel came with her father's sheep; for she kept them.

10 And it came to pass, when Jacob saw Rachel the daughter of Laban his mother's brother, and the sheep of Laban his mother's brother, that Jacob went near, and rolled the stone from the well's mouth, and watered the flock of Laban his mother's brother.

11 And Jacob kissed Rachel, and lifted up his voice, and wept.

12 And Jacob told Rachel that he was her father's brother, and that he was Rebekah's son: and she ran and told her father.

¹³ And it came to pass, when Laban heard the tidings of Jacob his sister's son, that he ran to meet him, and embraced him, and kissed him, and brought him to his house. And he told Laban all these things.

¹⁴ And Laban said to him, Surely thou art my bone and my flesh. And he abode with him the space of a month.

¹⁵ And Laban said unto Jacob, Because thou art my brother, shouldest thou therefore serve me for nought? tell me, what shall thy wages be?

¹⁶ And Laban had two daughters: the name of the elder was Leah, and the name of the younger was Rachel.

¹⁷ Leah was tender eyed; but Rachel was beautiful and well favoured.

¹⁸ And Jacob loved Rachel; and said, I will serve thee seven years for Rachel thy younger daughter.

¹⁹ And Laban said, It is better that I give her to thee, than that I should give her to another man: abide with me.

²⁰ And Jacob served seven years for Rachel; and they seemed unto him but a few days, for the love he had to her.

²¹ And Jacob said unto Laban, Give me my wife, for my days are fulfilled, that I may go in unto her.

²² And Laban gathered together all the men of the place, and made a feast.

²³ And it came to pass in the evening, that he took Leah his daughter, and brought her to him; and he went in unto her.

²⁴ And Laban gave unto his daughter Leah Zilpah his maid for an handmaid.

²⁵ And it came to pass, that in the morning, behold, it was Leah: and he said to Laban, What is this thou hast done unto me? did not I serve with thee for Rachel? wherefore then hast thou beguiled me?

²⁶ And Laban said, It must not be so done in our country, to give the younger before the firstborn.

²⁷ Fulfil her week, and we will give thee this also for the service which thou shalt serve with me yet seven other years.

28 And Jacob did so, and fulfilled her week: and he gave him Rachel his daughter to wife also.

29 And Laban gave to Rachel his daughter Bilhah his handmaid to be her maid.

30 And he went in also unto Rachel, and he loved also Rachel more than Leah, and served with him yet seven other years.

31 And when the LORD saw that Leah was hated, he opened her womb: but Rachel was barren.

32 And Leah conceived, and bare a son, and she called his name Reuben: for she said, Surely the LORD hath looked upon my affliction; now therefore my husband will love me.

33 And she conceived again, and bare a son; and said, Because the LORD hath heard I was hated, he hath therefore given me this son also: and she called his name Simeon.

34 And she conceived again, and bare a son; and said, Now this time will my husband be joined unto me, because I have born him three sons: therefore was his name called Levi.

35 And she conceived again, and bare a son: and she said, Now will I praise the LORD: therefore she called his name Judah; and left bearing.

Jacob was deceived into marrying Leah, when he obviously wanted her sister Rachel! Did Jacob divorce or leave Leah? No he did not, although he rejected Leah for Rachel!

Leah had children with Jacob, so they were obviously meant to be married, although it began out of deception.

Divorce in Hebrew=H3748=Ker-ee-thooth=Cutting of the marital bond.

THE MOST HIGH fuses two together as one, and it hurts, very badly for that one unit to become 2 separate parts! Note: Separation is temporal and oftentimes divinely necessary. Surgery hurts (separation, cutting away), and it takes time to heal, and once healing is done, you can get back to business! Marriage needs to be viewed this way, instead of divorce! Spouses suffer from divorce, children suffer from divorce, the community suffers from divorce, (last thing we need is more broken homes!) The only ones that benefit, and benefit well from divorce, are divorce lawyers! I must be TRUTHFUL....I felt as if I was dying when my wife said that she wanted to divorce me, and holding those papers, I was served was like me holding a pronounced death sentence! It was not because my wife was my idol, it was because spending 16 years with the same woman, and not seeing the fact that this was coming was devasting!

Di-vorce is a Di-viding of a force!

I CORINTHIANS 7:15

15 But if the unbelieving depart, let him depart. A brother or a sister is not under bondage in such cases: but God hath called us to peace.
Unbelieveing=G571=Ap-is-tos=Infidel, unbeliever.
At least one believer should be fasting and praying to save the marriage!
Divorce should be avoided by all means, in these days and times, marriage is a reflection of The Messiah's relationship with his covenant people!

JEREMIAH 3:1-22

They say, If a man put away his wife, and she go from him, and become another man's, shall he return unto her again? shall not that land be greatly polluted? but thou hast played the harlot with many lovers; yet return again to me, saith the LORD.

2 Lift up thine eyes unto the high places, and see where thou hast not been lien with. In the ways hast thou sat for them, as the Arabian in the wilderness; and thou hast polluted the land with thy whoredoms and with thy wickedness.

3 Therefore the showers have been withholden, and there hath been no latter rain; and thou hadst a whore's forehead, thou refusedst to be ashamed.

4 Wilt thou not from this time cry unto me, My father, thou art the guide of my youth?

5 Will he reserve his anger for ever? will he keep it to the end? Behold, thou hast spoken and done evil things as thou couldest.

6 The LORD said also unto me in the days of Josiah the king, Hast thou seen that which backsliding Israel hath done? she is gone up upon every high mountain and under every green tree, and there hath played the harlot.

7 And I said after she had done all these things, Turn thou unto me. But she returned not. And her treacherous sister Judah saw it.

8 And I saw, when for all the causes whereby backsliding Israel committed adultery I had put her away, and given her a bill of divorce; yet her treacherous sister Judah feared not, but went and played the harlot also.

9 And it came to pass through the lightness of her whoredom, that she defiled the land, and committed adultery with stones and with stocks.

10 And yet for all this her treacherous sister Judah hath not turned unto me with her whole heart, but feignedly, saith the LORD.

11 And the LORD said unto me, The backsliding Israel hath justified herself more than treacherous Judah.

12 Go and proclaim these words toward the north, and say, Return, thou backsliding Israel, saith the LORD; and I will not cause mine anger to fall upon you: for I am merciful, saith the LORD, and I will not keep anger for ever.

13 Only acknowledge thine iniquity, that thou hast transgressed against the LORD thy God, and hast scattered thy ways to the strangers under every green tree, and ye have not obeyed my voice, saith the LORD.

14 Turn, O backsliding children, saith the LORD; for I am married unto you: and I will take you one of a city, and two of a family, and I will bring you to Zion:

15 And I will give you pastors according to mine heart, which shall feed you with knowledge and understanding.

16 And it shall come to pass, when ye be multiplied and increased in the land, in those days, saith the LORD, they shall say no more, The ark of the covenant of the LORD: neither shall it come to mind: neither shall they remember it; neither shall they visit it; neither shall that be done any more.

17 At that time they shall call Jerusalem the throne of the LORD; and all the nations shall be gathered unto it, to the name of the LORD, to Jerusalem: neither shall they walk any more after the imagination of their evil heart.

18 In those days the house of Judah shall walk with the house of Israel, and they shall come together out of the land of the north to the land that I have given for an inheritance unto your fathers.

19 But I said, How shall I put thee among the children, and give thee a pleasant land, a goodly heritage of the hosts of nations? and I said, Thou shalt call me, My father; and shalt not turn away from me.

20 Surely as a wife treacherously departeth from her husband, so have ye dealt treacherously with me, O house of Israel, saith the LORD.

21 A voice was heard upon the high places, weeping and supplications of the children of Israel: for they have perverted their way, and they have forgotten the LORD their God.

22 Return, ye backsliding children, and I will heal your backslidings. Behold, we come unto thee; for thou art the LORD our God.

[THE CREATOR HIMSELF, had to divorce his "Wives" {Yes "Wives", Israel & Judah!}, and if you notice, he tried to work it out with them, and they refused, choosing to continue in unfaithfulness to HIM so he had to put them away for a reason & a season, and as we see all will be right again, with his Chosen nation of people!]

HOSEA 2:1-23

Say ye unto your brethren, Ammi; and to your sisters, Ruhamah.

2 Plead with your mother, plead: for she is not my wife, neither am I her husband: let her therefore put away her whoredoms out of her sight, and her adulteries from between her breasts;

3 Lest I strip her naked, and set her as in the day that she was born, and make her as a wilderness, and set her like a dry land, and slay her with thirst.

4 And I will not have mercy upon her children; for they be the children of whoredoms.

5 For their mother hath played the harlot: she that conceived them hath done shamefully: for she said, I will go after my lovers, that give me my bread and my water, my wool and my flax, mine oil and my drink.

6 Therefore, behold, I will hedge up thy way with thorns, and make a wall, that she shall not find her paths.

7 And she shall follow after her lovers, but she shall not overtake them; and she shall seek them, but shall not find them: then shall she say, I will go and return to my first husband; for then was it better with me than now.

8 For she did not know that I gave her corn, and wine, and oil, and multiplied her silver and gold, which they prepared for Baal.

9 Therefore will I return, and take away my corn in the time thereof, and my wine in the season thereof, and will recover my wool and my flax given to cover her nakedness.

10 And now will I discover her lewdness in the sight of her lovers, and none shall deliver her out of mine hand.

11 I will also cause all her mirth to cease, her feast days, her new moons, and her sabbaths, and all her solemn feasts.

12 And I will destroy her vines and her fig trees, whereof she hath said, These are my rewards that my lovers have given me: and I will make them a forest, and the beasts of the field shall eat them.

13 And I will visit upon her the days of Baalim, wherein she burned incense to them, and she decked herself with her earrings and her jewels, and she went after her lovers, and forgat me, saith the LORD.

14 Therefore, behold, I will allure her, and bring her into the wilderness, and speak comfortably unto her.

15 And I will give her her vineyards from thence, and the valley of Achor for a door of hope: and she shall sing there, as in the days of her youth, and as in the day when she came up out of the land of Egypt.

16 And it shall be at that day, saith the LORD, that thou shalt call me Ishi; and shalt call me no more Baali.

17 For I will take away the names of Baalim out of her mouth, and they shall no more be remembered by their name.

18 And in that day will I make a covenant for them with the beasts of the field and with the fowls of heaven, and with the creeping things of the ground: and I will break the bow and the sword and the battle out of the earth, and will make them to lie down safely.

19 And I will betroth thee unto me for ever; yea, I will betroth thee unto me in righteousness, and in judgment, and in lovingkindness, and in mercies.

20 I will even betroth thee unto me in faithfulness: and thou shalt know the LORD.

21 And it shall come to pass in that day, I will hear, saith the LORD, I will hear the heavens, and they shall hear the earth;

22 And the earth shall hear the corn, and the wine, and the oil; and they shall hear Jezreel.

23 And I will sow her unto me in the earth; and I will have mercy upon her that had not obtained mercy; and I will say to them which were not my people, Thou art my people; and they shall say, Thou art my God.

[The only example of a perfect marriage, is THE CREATOR's marriage with his chosen, elect people! HE is perfect we are not, and as we see HE has been patient with his bride, so men, we have to follow this same example! Ladie's let this be an example, of the love and patience that your husband show's, don't take advantage! Love and Reverence Him, his love and patience towards you is not weakness, by no means! Chosen men such as myself, we are constantly getting "Better" not "Bitter", so I know from experience that a "Better" man is nowhere near as attractive to some women as a "Bitter" man! The "Better" man will lead his woman into some beautiful things if she sticks it out with him, and The "Bitter" man that starts off exciting, will eventually lead that woman into destruction! I have seen it, I know it, and I'm not retracting it!] - Period

CHAPTER FOUR (4)
INSTITUTION OF PERSECUTION

II TIMOTHY 3:10-12

[10] But thou hast fully known my doctrine, manner of life, purpose, faith, longsuffering, charity, patience,

[11] Persecutions, afflictions, which came unto me at Antioch, at Iconium, at Lystra; what persecutions I endured: but out of them all the Lord delivered me.

[12] Yea, and all that will live godly in Christ Jesus shall suffer persecution.

I'm an educated man, and this is not something I walk around with as a badge of honor and being in expectancy of others to acknowledge me in any formality sense. I have worked hard on my education, for the simple fact that I want to learn, and I want to know The TRUTH. I can only be who and what I was created to be!

ROMANS 9:20-24

[20] Nay but, O man, who art thou that repliest against God? Shall the thing formed say to him that formed it, Why hast thou made me thus?

[21] Hath not the potter power over the clay, of the same lump to make one vessel unto honour, and another unto dishonour?

[22] What if God, willing to shew his wrath, and to make his power known, endured with much longsuffering the vessels of wrath fitted to destruction:

[23] And that he might make known the riches of his glory on the vessels of mercy, which he had afore prepared unto glory,

[24] Even us, whom he hath called, not of the Jews only, but also of the Gentiles?

As I spoke of in the prelude, I have earned a Doctorate Degree in Business Administration, that I earned in the year of 2016. I have been studying business since the year 1998, and I started at a Business College (that I won't name, although they did me and others faulty! I now have a heart for the younger generation, to learn a trade and be done right, to prepare them for the future) and I wanted to continue my education from there, although my first born child was born 2 months after I had graduated, and I let others talk me out of continuing my education since I was now a daddy. (It was a mistake, listening to others, because I was working full time and going to college full time, I have always been blessed to multi-task like that, to the jealousy and envy of many).

List of my Educational Credentials:

COMPUTER APPLICATIONS IN BUSINESS – **BUSINESS CERTIFICATION -1998**
WRITTEN AND ORAL COMMUNICATIONS – **ASSOCIATE'S DEGREE – 2005**
BUSINESS LEADERSHIP – **BUSINESS CERTIFICATION - 2007**
BUSINESS ADMINISTRATION – **BACHELOR'S DEGREE - 2010**
BUSINESS ADMINSTRATION – **MASTER'S DEGREE - 2012**
BUSINESS ADMINISTRATION – **DOCTRATE DEGREE – 2016**

All of this education above is to be used to glorify THE MOST HIGH and not myself, know one else, or even the company. All of the above education was not in vain, being educated has taught me a lot, especially realizing that a lot of it was mis-education!

Also several people think that I'm too bold or too crazy to tell other people this; who cares though, I always feel moved to tell people this......all the above education was accomplished by a man that had to do an extra year of high school! Yes, I was a High School Senior not once, but twice! [1988-1989] Why? I'm not justifying it, it's just that...
I was involved in a lot of fights, DUE TO BEING BULLIED.
I was scared to go to class, DUE TO BEING BULLIED.
I played sick and didn't go to school much, DUE TO BEING BULLIED.
I didn't pay attention to scheduled home work, DUE TO BEING BULLIED.

Yes, I was bullied from elementary school, to junior high school (middle school), on up to High School. I was bullied on the school bus, walking to school, in school all day, and back on the bus, or walking home from school.
When I attended High School my second senior year, I was laughed at, at first, and then I started getting respect from my peers! I believe they respected the courage that it took, for me to agree to endure what I had to endure to receive my High School diploma.
I must admit that when I attended Business College 9 years later, I did not receive any bullying, although I was in a relationship expecting for my first born child to be born, I was very popular with the ladies! I didn't cheat physically, but I sure cheated mentally!
[The chosen have a built in loyalty about them, to want to do right, even before they have the required "Born-Again" experience. The loyalty I'm talking about gets the chosen in trouble, sometimes when they are loyal to the wrong people, and/or that loyalty is used to ignore "red flags" that are being shown to them]
Working on receiving my Associate's degree all the way up to receiving my Doctorate degree was a totally different case! I was bullied from day one, receiving my Associates degree, the moment I stepped onto the campus! It took me 3.5 years to earn my Associates degree and when I was ready to graduate, I lie not................
They said the computer system was ruined due to a gas explosion, and they had lost all records of me, even being in attendance at the school! I was told I could not graduate, with no record of me being in attendance, at the school! I fought and fought hard, and I not only graduated, I was asked, to pray at the graduation commencement!

MATTHEW 23:1-10

Then spake Jesus to the multitude, and to his disciples,

2 Saying The scribes and the Pharisees sit in Moses' seat:

3 All therefore whatsoever they bid you observe, that observe and do; but do not ye after their works: for they say, and do not.

4 For they bind heavy burdens and grievous to be borne, and lay them on men's shoulders; but they themselves will not move them with one of their fingers.

5 But all their works they do for to be seen of men: they make broad their phylacteries, and enlarge the borders of their garments,

6 And love the uppermost rooms at feasts, and the chief seats in the synagogues,

7 And greetings in the markets, and to be called of men, Rabbi, Rabbi.

8 But be not ye called Rabbi: for one is your Master, even Christ; and all ye are brethren.

9 And call no man your father upon the earth: for one is your Father, which is in heaven.

10 Neither be ye called masters: for one is your Master, even Christ.

Master={from verse 10 above}=G2519=Kath-ayg-ay-tace=A teacher.

A Doctor, or someone whom holds a "Doctorate" degree is also known as a teacher, so I know that the question is this for me, why do I call myself a doctor, although I do have an earned degree, although The Messiah prohibits and commands for no man to be called master {teacher}! Well, I'm glad you asked!

The Dr in front of my name is an acronym which means "discipline required". I sought The CREATOR on this and this is what he spoke back to me! So no I'm not in a rebellious, sinful, opposition to The Living WORD, I'm being obedient, to what I asked!

I must add that I don't get caught up on titles, at all!
I'm just as comfortable spending time with someone on WELFARE,
As I am comfortable spending time with a MILLIONAIRE!
A title is just a title! Everyone has a title.......
EITHER YOU'RE A **SAINT** OR YOU'RE AN **AIN'T!**

We have to use discernment because we can't trust neither! Sadly, ain'ts are more real!

CHAPTER FIVE (5)
<u>ENTREPRENEUR</u>, THAT MUST REMAIN <u>PURE!</u>
<u>PSALMS 106:34-39</u>

³⁴ They did not destroy the nations, concerning whom the LORD commanded them:

³⁵ But were mingled among the heathen, and learned their works.

³⁶ And they served their idols: which were a snare unto them.

³⁷ Yea, they sacrificed their sons and their daughters unto devils,

³⁸ And shed innocent blood, even the blood of their sons and of their daughters, whom they sacrificed unto the idols of Canaan: and the land was polluted with blood.

³⁹ Thus were they defiled with their own works, and went a whoring with their own inventions.

No matter how many businesses I have my name attached to, and no matter what type or classification the business is, I'm not an owner of the business at all, I'm merely a Business Steward! Man is going to recognize me as an Entrepreneur, and instead of wasting time and energy explaining, I'm just leaving it here in this book, that I'm merely a steward!

Before anything else, I'm a Man of The MOST HIGH and that's before me being a preacher, a husband, a daddy, a son, a brother, a uncle, a brother-in-law, a son-in-law, a friend, and a business man.
As a Man of The MOST HIGH, I must remain pure before HIM and true to HIM, and in fellowship with HIM and in obedience to HIM!
It get's lonely often, I would be a liar if I said other wise, A chosen vessel must understand that they cannot majority of the time, be around other people!
A chosen vessel should not, be the life of the party, because a chosen vessel should not be at that party in the first place! Please don't get me wrong, I'm not saying or implying that a chosen vessel cannot or should not enjoy themselves! There has to be a balance!
<u>PROVERBS 20:23</u>
²³ Divers weights are an abomination unto the LORD; and a false balance is not good.

As a Man of The MOST HIGH I must always pray before being invited to go anyplace. {True story}: My wife and I were invited to a graduation for a ex-church member that was graduating from college. My wife and I attended and as soon as we arrived other, ex-church members arrived and they all started whispering about Us being there, and who invited us? After this died down, then everything seemed okay, until I was asked

to deejay. I started deejaying (I used to be a deejay in my B.M. Before Messiah days) and I was congratulated on the job I was doing, then.......a woman that laughed at me praising The MOST HIGH back when we attended the same church, came up to me and said in front of everybody "He went from a deejay, to a preacher, and from a preacher back to a deejay!" As she said this and laughed I told her "no, no, no there has to be a balance in a man's life!" Nobody responded once I said that, and you know what............
I was sending a bad message, by even being there! Now people are going to talk and put their two cents in, even when it's not asked for, there is no getting around it!
As a chosen vessel, you are going to be very scrutinized and if you are falsely accused that's one thing; however if you are guilty as charged, there is a price to pay!

: I THESSALONIANS 5:22
22 Abstain from all appearance of evil.
Now a prime example of being falsely accused

LUKE 7:33-35
33 For John the Baptist came neither eating bread nor drinking wine; and ye say, He hath a devil.
34 The Son of man is come eating and drinking; and ye say, Behold a gluttonous man, and a winebibber, a friend of publicans and sinners!
35 But wisdom is justified of all her children.
[As we see, John the Baptist was accused of having a devil, and he didn't even come in the public's eye, and here it is The Messiah a perfect, sinless man is accused of being a glutton and a wino, just because he is eating on a public feast day, & drinking wine.]

ECCLESIASTES 10:19
19 A feast is made for laughter, and wine maketh merry: but money answereth all things.

A. REASONS WHY THE CHOSEN NEED TO BE SECLUDED	B. REASONS WHY THE CHOSEN SHOULD NOT BE SECLUDED	SCRIPTURAL PROOF
THE CHOSEN CANNOT, AND WILL NOT HEAR FROM THE MOST HIGH WHEN THEY ARE AROUND OTHERS	THE CHOSEN DO HAVE TO BE AROUND OTHERS AS PART OF THEIR MISSION, PURPOSE, AND TO BLESS OTHERS	A. MATTHEW 14:22-23 B. JOHN 7:4-18

A. MATTHEW 14:22-23
22 And straightway Jesus constrained his disciples to get into a ship, and to go before him unto the other side, while he sent the multitudes away.
23 And when he had sent the multitudes away, he went up into a mountain apart to pray: and when the evening was come, he was there alone.

B. JOHN 7:4-18
4 For there is no man that doeth any thing in secret, and he himself seeketh to be known openly. If thou do these things, shew thyself to the world.
5 For neither did his brethren believe in him.
6 Then Jesus said unto them, My time is not yet come: but your time is alway ready.

7 The world cannot hate you; but me it hateth, because I testify of it, that the works thereof are evil.

8 Go ye up unto this feast: I go not up yet unto this feast: for my time is not yet full come.

9 When he had said these words unto them, he abode still in Galilee.

10 But when his brethren were gone up, then went he also up unto the feast, not openly, but as it were in secret.

11 Then the Jews sought him at the feast, and said, Where is he?

12 And there was much murmuring among the people concerning him: for some said, He is a good man: others said, Nay; but he deceiveth the people.

13 Howbeit no man spake openly of him for fear of the Jews.

14 Now about the midst of the feast Jesus went up into the temple, and taught.

15 And the Jews marvelled, saying, How knoweth this man letters, having never learned?

16 Jesus answered them, and said, My doctrine is not mine, but his that sent me.

17 If any man will do his will, he shall know of the doctrine, whether it be of God, or whether I speak of myself.

18 He that speaketh of himself seeketh his own glory: but he that seeketh his glory that sent him, the same is true, and no unrighteousness is in him.

[As a business man, I have to remain disciplined, and I do things (that I won't share with anyone, it's between me and my CREATOR) daily, and will always do daily. I have been called a routine man and that is boring to some; however it's what has allowed me to be elevated, because it is part of being obedient to THE MOST HIGH all the rest of my days!]

[I also, will share this, The Chosen, (I should have stressed this in previous chapters, when I speak of The Chosen, I'm talking about The Chosen ones that follow The GOD of Abraham, Issac, and Jacob, not those that call themselves The Chosen and they "choose" to follow anything or anyone other than The CREATOR of all things visible and invisible) need to, and should continue to fast! Fasting is a spiritual discipline, that all believers should be doing, The Chosen on the other hand are much closer to THE MOST HIGH and their daily, weekly, monthly, yearly, and lifetime purpose on the planet Earth has to be clear. Evil is always seeking to snuff out The Chosen, so for their own protection and as their own responsibility, The Chosen need to stay fasting, and must embrace it as a lifestyle. I know certain people that cannot fast due to having health complications, and I believe this to be the work of The devil! The last thing The devil wants is for a chosen vessel to fast, and as a result gain spiritual strength and insight! The Chosen must fast, it is not optional!]

PSALMS 109:24

24 My knees are weak through fasting; and my flesh faileth of fatness.

[Notice he says that his knees are weak through fasting, why? He had not eaten, and this is the reason also why he said that his flesh faileth of fatness, see he had lost weight from not eating. I must stress this, because so many born-again believers today, stress that you can fast from television, music, reading etc. None of this is Biblical!]

ACTS 9:8-9,17-19

8 And Saul arose from the earth; and when his eyes were opened, he saw no man: but they led him by the hand, and brought him into Damascus.

9 And he was three days without sight, and neither did eat nor drink.

17 And Ananias went his way, and entered into the house; and putting his hands on him said, Brother Saul, the Lord, even Jesus, that appeared unto thee in the way as thou camest, hath sent me, that thou mightest receive thy sight, and be filled with the Holy Ghost.

18 And immediately there fell from his eyes as it had been scales: and he received sight forthwith, and arose, and was baptized.

19 And when he had received meat, he was strengthened. Then was Saul certain days with the disciples which were at Damascus.

[This was clearly Saul fasting for 3 days, talking to The Deliverer while he was fasting and receiving instructions on his future purposed mission!]

MATTHEW 4:1-4, 11

Then was Jesus led up of the Spirit into the wilderness to be tempted of the devil.

2 And when he had fasted forty days and forty nights, he was afterward an hungred.

3 And when the tempter came to him, he said, If thou be the Son of God, command that these stones be made bread.

4 But he answered and said, It is written, Man shall not live by bread alone, but by every word that proceedeth out of the mouth of God.

11 Then the devil leaveth him, and, behold, angels came and ministered unto him.

The Messiah was hungry {from fasting], and angels ministered {served him food after}

CHAPTER SIX (6)
<u>VISION</u> WITH ABSOLUTE <u>PRECISION!</u>

<u>HABAKKUK 2:1-2</u>

I will stand upon my watch, and set me upon the tower, and will watch to see what he will say unto me, and what I shall answer when I am reproved.

2 And the LORD answered me, and said, Write the vision, and make it plain upon tables, that he may run that readeth it.

Tue, Sep 30, 2014 at 12:55 PM

Hi Martin,

Sorry to take so long getting back to you. That is a quite an interesting idea you have. Let me talk to a few grant makers I know and see what they have to say. Take care.

Tue, Oct 7, 2014 at 5:47 PM

I am not trying to bug you by any means. I am contacting you today to see if possibly you have heard from any grant makers yet, concerning this much needed, unique business idea. Please contact me back at your convenience.

Thank You For Your Time,

Martin Bryant

Wed, Oct 8, 2014 at 8:13 AM

Hi Martin,

So far I am drawing a blank as to funders. One of the main problems you will have is trying to meet all of the federal and state laws governing transportation. They make it almost impossible for a small service like the one you want to run. I have one more I am still trying to get in touch with.

The problem you may have though is meeting all their legal requirements.

I will be in touch if I hear of anything else.

{All 3 of these are real email messages, (now I did delete the personal name, of who I was communicating with of course) that I sent back in 2014. When I was first given the idea, vision, and plan to start a transportation business, named "Aged Not Caged". Funding was never made available for the business, and other factors came into play regarding a transportation company for seniors; however I always felt something in me, telling me not to give up, not to quit!

My daddy [wearing K.C. Chiefs hat] at the hospital on the morning when my first born, was born!

My Dad and I were very close, and it will be explained how he had a direct impact, influence, and was responsible for the idea and development of The MOST HIGH birthing this business through me!

My daddy passed away in the year 2013, about a year before I felt a strong compulsion to start a transportation company for seniors. My daddy was a retired military man, having joined the military at the age of 17. My dad was blessed to travel the world and was used to traveling the world, while he was in the military and he did some light travel when he was retired from the military. My daddy was diagnosed with cancer, and received chemotherapy treatment, and shortly after he was told that the cancer had went into remission. All of us (his family) celebrated, not realizing that a short time later in a matter of months, he was told that the cancer returned.

My daddies doctor told him, that if he desired to travel (which he did), that he would have to do so right away. We had all planned on traveling as a family, and unfortunately we never got the opportunity because my daddy passed away at a parade.

My daddies passing hit the family hard, and now my mother was a widow, and just as I was lead to say when I spoke at my daddies funeral, we needed prayer, especially my mama losing her husband of 58 years.

I was their for my mother, as best as possible; however I noticed quickly that my mama was not getting out like she should. My mother would go to the grocery store (my mother no longer drives) and other places that she needed to go; however my mother needed to get out the house for recreation not just for the sake of business. I know that I will get flack over this; however I'm never scared to speak the TRUTH, the church that my mama and daddy belonged to for years, surely wasn't there to get my mama out of the house, as they had promised! I made up my mind that I would do something to get my mama out of the house, and other seniors, no matter what the situation to get them out of the house also. I worked for a transportation company at the time, (same company that I returned to in the year of 2023) that specialized in transporting individuals with intellectually developmental disabilities along with those that were physically challenged. I was good at my job and I enjoyed my job, it's just that that's exactly what it was a job,(j.ust o.ver b.roke) and I always felt in my soul that I was destined for something different, that I actually would be a steward of.

I began doing diligent research on transportation companies for seniors and I kept on running into the same challenges and same dead ends, I had 5 years of experience, as a transporter and I had held a class B CDL for over 14 years at this point, so experience wasn't the issue, a proper business plan wasn't the issue, funding the business (the emails on the first page of this chapter, shows the proof in the pudding) was the issue! I have to be brutally honest, also their were many that were not keen, at all on helping a man of color start an LLC transportation company! Racism is real, and I'm not going to be silent about it, nor act like it doesn't exist, or that I never have or never do deal with it. I'm greatful though that those doors were closed, because since they were closed, I began looking and researching for another way to get seniors out. I was given the name "Aged Not Caged" divinely!(***Seniors deserve and have earned the right to enjoy a better quality of life, outside the bird cage, they deserve to fly free as a bird, hence the name Aged Not Caged***) I have been Blessed with the gift of being "Poetic" when I teach, the lesson titles rhyme, when I preach the sermon titles rhyme, as a business man, the name of the businesses and their services rhyme!

Why and how did Virtual Reality and Augmented Reality come into play?

I started to see that a transportation bus company was not for me, and personally for me, I did not want all the liability and responsibility that would come along with it. I would never knock the next man, or next woman, everything is not for everybody.
I still had the same passion to get seniors out, and about 4 years had passed since receiving the name of the company, and trying to implement the idea, and also I was no longer in the transportation industry, I passed the examination to sell life, health, and medical insurance with flying colors (Thanks be to you, Heavenly Father!) and I was working for an insurance company to where we had to enter into people's homes and majority of those people were senior citizens; which I connected with in a very special way! I talked with those seniors, and honestly it was not about me getting that insurance sell, it was about me keeping them company, and learning from them! I absolutely loved it and I couldn't wait for my scheduled visits, to check on my clients and to meet with new clients! I admit that I did get comfortable doing what I was doing and this is something that a chosen vessel, should never do! I learned that no matter what, you have to keep your focus on your GOD appointed purpose in life! I learned that although we can get experience from other pre-assignments in life, that we can never lose sight of our primary assignment [purpose] in life!
My experience in the insurance industry changed when the pandemic of the year 2020 hit North America. I know several people started utilizing Zoom, Google meet, Facetime etc, for insurance sells and it was not successful for me and here is the reason why.
Remember as I stated earlier, the majority of my insurance clients were seniors and those seniors did not want me to enter into their homes, even with a mask on for safety for them, and safety for me. (Who could have blamed them?)   My senior clients did not want to learn to use Zoom, Google meet, or Facetime either. My focus was back on my appointed purpose, and what I was anointed to do. I did have a relative, a auntie that I loved and miss dearly, and I remember how it was for her dealing with Alzheimer's and I noticed that my mama started to show signs of Alzheimer's setting on her early. Now I prayed that I could not only get my mama and other seniors out of the house, I also prayed that something could be done to lessen or cure her of Alzheimer's.
I researched and prayed, I prayed and researched and I was shown this......... Virtual Reality.
I thought that Virtual Reality was only for gaming, and boy was I wrong!
VR slows down the effects of Alzheimer's and Dementia, and helps prevent slips and falls, due to the fact mobility is increased utilizing VR. I also gave an Uber ride to a lady that told me out of the blue, to get involved with VR! I believe this lady could have been an angel in disguise, because she encouraged me in all ways, big time! I contacted some local businesses here in Kansas City, Missouri and I got in contact with the right one, and my team and myself, started experiencing VR for ourselves and we allowed my mother, my brother and a woman whom is now a good friend of mine, as well as my sister in Messiah that's a cancer patient.

Aged Not Caged is all about bringing unique change too ways of doing things that we are not used to! In other words, the research we do, is way outside of the box!

SERVICES THAT AGED NOT CAGED OFFERS:

NAME OF SERVICE:	WHAT SERVICE IS:	UNIQUENESS OF IT:
Tours 4u & **Yours**	VR trips for seniors	We create our own programs
Load The last **Episode**	Trips for terminal, foretold persons, & hospice patients	We create programs designed to individuals specifications
Mo **Learning** Mo **Burning**	A learning institute and trade school	We educate, train, & employ students!
Birds carry **Words**	Recorded poetry , to music produced by engineers	Teaches people to speak life and not death
Nutritive 2 **Live**	An in-house cafeteria, serving healthy home grown food	The cafeteria serves the public and it's students and employees
N'durance Assurance	A new sport!	Nothing like this has been done & recognized as a sport before
Fishes N2 **Wishes**	Allows the developmentally disabled to experience VR	This service will always leave a lasting impact
Pulley The **Bulley**	Therapy for victims of bullying	This service will forever change, how bullying has been treated
Neva-Fakers- Care-takers	Concierge service for seniors	What we offer with the concierge service is original
Deposit Closet	A brand new invention!	An invention that is original, and will soon be everywhere!
Right-**Thare** Day-**Care**	In house day care	A daycare for employees, and students!

We offer all 11 of the above services, with all sincerity and all Love, to people in all places and of all races!

CHAPTER SEVEN (7)
HAS THE COLOR RED, GONE TO THIS MAN'S HEAD?

JASHER 55:12-13

12 And when Jacob approached the camp of Joseph, Jacob observed the camp that was coming toward him with Joseph, and it gratified him and Jacob was astonished at it.

13 And Jacob said unto Judah, Who is that man whom I see in the camp of Egypt dressed in kingly robes with a very red garment upon him and a royal crown upon his head, who has alighted from his chariot and is coming toward us? and Judah answered his father, saying, He is thy son Joseph the king; and Jacob rejoiced in seeing the glory of his son.

[Notice it says, a very red garment, Jacob noticed that a very red garment represented royalty, what he did not recognize is that the royal person in the very red garment was his long lost son!]

When The Bible mentions Scarlet, does it really mean purple?

PROVERBS 31:10-22

10 Who can find a virtuous woman? for her price is far above rubies.

11 The heart of her husband doth safely trust in her, so that he shall have no need of spoil.

12 She will do him good and not evil all the days of her life.

13 She seeketh wool, and flax, and worketh willingly with her hands.

14 She is like the merchants' ships; she bringeth her food from afar.

15 She riseth also while it is yet night, and giveth meat to her household, and a portion to her maidens.

16 She considereth a field, and buyeth it: with the fruit of her hands she planteth a vineyard.

17 She girdeth her loins with strength, and strengtheneth her arms.

18 She perceiveth that her merchandise is good: her candle goeth not out by night.

19 She layeth her hands to the spindle, and her hands hold the distaff.

20 She stretcheth out her hand to the poor; yea, she reacheth forth her hands to the needy.

21 She is not afraid of the snow for her household: for all her household are clothed with scarlet.

22 She maketh herself coverings of tapestry; her clothing is silk and purple.

Scarlet=H8144=Verse 21=Shaw-nee=Crimson, scarlet.
Purple=H713=Verse 22=Ar-gaw-mawn=Purple.
{So as we can see Scarlet and Purple are both used a verse apart and they are both 2 different Hebrew words, for 2 different colors!}

MATTHEW 27:27-29

27 Then the soldiers of the governor took Jesus into the common hall, and gathered unto him the whole band of soldiers.

28 And they stripped him, and put on him a scarlet robe.

29 And when they had platted a crown of thorns, they put it upon his head, and a reed in his right hand: and they bowed the knee before him, and mocked him, saying, Hail, King of the Jews!

[Scarlet=G2847=Kok-kee-nos=Crimson colored.][3 examples, are any of them evil?]

REVELATION 12:3

3 And there appeared another wonder in heaven; and behold a great red dragon, having seven heads and ten horns, and seven crowns upon his heads.
RED=VERSE 3= G4450=Poor-hros=Fire like, that is flame colored.

Fire like is orangish in color, not blood red, brick red, cherry red, candy apple red, etc!
What 2 colors make purple? Purple is made from Red and Blue. So most people recognize purple as the only color of royalty; however you can't make purple without red!
Red is not of the devil, that is a man-made superstition and a tradition!
In the King James version of The Bible the word Blood is mentioned about 369 times.
What other color do you know of that blood is?

LEVITICUS 17:11

11 For the life of the flesh is in the blood: and I have given it to you upon the altar to make an atonement for your souls: for it is the blood that maketh an atonement for the soul.

HEBREWS 13:11-12

11 For the bodies of those beasts, whose blood is brought into the sanctuary by the high priest for sin, are burned without the camp.
12 Wherefore Jesus also, that he might sanctify the people with his own blood, suffered without the gate.

REVELATION 1:5

5 And from Jesus Christ, who is the faithful witness, and the first begotten of the dead, and the prince of the kings of the earth. Unto him that loved us, and washed us from our sins in his own blood,

6 And hath made us kings and priests unto God and his Father; to him be glory and dominion for ever and ever. Amen.

REVELATION 12:10-11

10 And I heard a loud voice saying in heaven, Now is come salvation, and strength, and the kingdom of our God, and the power of his Christ: for the accuser of our brethren is cast down, which accused them before our God day and night.

11 And they overcame him by the blood of the Lamb, and by the word of their testimony; and they loved not their lives unto the death.

[Without blood which of course is red, their would be no hope, no remission of sins, no atonement of sins, no deliverance, and no salvation! Tell me what does the devil have to do with the color red again????????]

THE COLOR RED	REPRESENTS:
	LOVE
	JOY
	COURAGE
	AGGRESSION
	SACRIFICE
	ATTENTION
	STRENGTH
	SEXUALITY
	VIBRANCY
	HEALING (BURNS OUT DISEASE)
	CREATIVITY
	PHYSICAL ENERGY
	CONFIDENCE
	PASSION IN RELATIONSHIPS
	STABILITY
	SURVIVAL
	POWER

SO WHY DO I WEAR THE COLOR RED, SO OFTEN?
I HAVE BEEN INSTRUCTED TO WEAR THE COLOR RED, STRAIGHT FROM HEAVEN, SO I'M OBEDIENT TO WHAT I HAVE BEEN INSTRUCTED!

I LIKE FOOTBALL, SPECIFICALLY THE NFL, I WAS BORN AND RAISED IN KANSAS CITY HOME OF THE:
- SUPERBOWL IV CHAMPIONS-[Kansas City Chiefs]
- SUPERBOWL LIV CHAMPIONS–[Kansas City Chiefs]
- SUPERBOWL LVII CHAMPIONS-[Kansas City Chiefs]

SO OBVIOUSLY THIS IS A NATURAL REASON FOR ME WEARING RED SO OFTEN!
I PROMISE I'M NOT A GANG-BANGER, REPRESENTING MY COLORS, EITHER!
I BELIEVE IN BEING OBEDIENT, AND I BELIEVE IN BEING DIFFERENT, I DARE TO BE DIFFERENT IN A WAY, THAT IS NOT SHOWING AN APPEARANCE OF EVIL OR OF SIN, SO ANYONE THAT IS OFFENDED, OR GETS OFFENDED BY HOW I DRESS MYSELF, IT'S YOUR PROBLEM AND NOT MINE!

CHAPTER EIGHT (8)
THE NEGATIVE **PARROT**, MY SEEDS WON'T **INHERIT!**

PROVERBS 18:21
21 Death and life are in the power of the tongue: and they that love it shall eat the fruit thereof.

WE SPEAK WHAT WE GET, WE GET WHAT WE SPEAK!

THE CHOSEN NEED TO BE MINDFUL OF WHAT THEY ARE THINKING, BECAUSE THOSE THOUGHTS BECOME WORDS, AND WORDS ARE POWERFUL THAT EVENTUALLY MANIFEST!

ANOTHER REASON WHY THE CHOSEN NEED TO BE ISOLATED MORE OFTEN THAN LESS OFTEN!

THIS MIGHT SOUND STRANGE BUT I ONCE HAD A PARROT THAT I COULD NOT SEE, AND I DIDN'T NEED TO FEED IT WITH FOOD, OR GIVE IT WATER TO DRINK. I WOULD SPEAK THINGS AND THAT PARROT WOULD REPEAT THOSE WORDS, AND THEN I WOULD END UP REPEATING WHAT THE PARROT SAID, AND WOULD START THE CYCLE ALL OVER AGAIN. I WILL NOT GIVE THESE PARROT TO MY SEEDS [CHILDREN], AND I'M STARVING THAT PARROT BY NOT GVING IT ANY NEGATIVE WORDS TO FEED ON!

MOST OF MY LIFE, I WAS RAISED TO BELIEVE THAT IF I SPOKE POSITIVE, OR IF I CLAIMED VICTORY, THEN I WAS BEING BRAGADOSIS!
NOT TRUE, AND I FOUND THAT OUT THE HARD WAY IN LIFE!

I'M TEACHING ALL OF MY YOUNGER CHILDREN, TO SPEAK LIFE, AND TO SPEAK LIFE OVER THEMSELVES AND OVER OTHERS.
WHEN WE SPEAK LIFE, WE ARE ALSO BRINGING GLORYING, OR GIVING GLORY TO THE GIVER OF LIFE.
ONE OF MANY THINGS, I HAVE HAD TO LEARN IS THAT WE CAN'T TRUST IN THE WORD OF MAN, WHEN YOU TRUST IN MAN, WE ARE LISTENING TO THAT PARROT!

JASHER 46:1-20

1 In those days Joseph was still confined in the prison house in the land of Egypt.

2 At that time the attendants of Pharaoh were standing before him, the chief of the butlers and the chief of the bakers which belonged to the king of Egypt.

3 And the butler took wine and placed it before the king to drink, and the baker placed bread before the king to eat, and the king drank of the wine and ate of the bread, he and his servants and ministers that ate at the king's table.

4 And whilst they were eating and drinking, the butler and the baker remained there, and Pharaoh's ministers found many flies in the wine, which the butler had brought, and stones of nitre were found in the baker's bread.

5 And the captain of the guard placed Joseph as an attendant on Pharaoh's officers, and Pharaoh's officers were in confinement one year.

6 And at the end of the year, they both dreamed dreams in one night, in the place of confinement where they were, and in the morning Joseph came to them to attend upon them as usual, and he saw them, and behold their countenances were dejected and sad.

7 And Joseph asked them, Why are your countenances sad and dejected this day? and they said unto him, We dreamed a dream, and there is no one to interpret it; and Joseph said unto them, Relate, I pray you, your dream unto me, and God shall give you an answer of peace as you desire.

8 And the butler related his dream unto Joseph, and he said, I saw in my dream, and behold a large vine was before me, and upon that vine I saw three branches, and the vine speedily blossomed and reached a great height, and its clusters were ripened and became grapes.

9 And I took the grapes and pressed them in a cup, and placed it in Pharaoh's hand and he drank; and Joseph said unto him, The three branches that were upon the vine are three days.

10 Yet within three days, the king will order thee to be brought out and he will restore thee to thy office, and thou shalt give the king his wine to drink as at first when thou wast his butler; but let me find favor in thy sight, that thou shalt remember me to Pharaoh when it will be well with thee, and do kindness unto me, and get me brought forth from this prison, for I was stolen away from the land of Canaan and was sold for a slave in this place.

11 And also that which was told thee concerning my master's wife is false, for they placed me in this dungeon for naught; and the butler answered Joseph, saying, If the king deal well with me as at first, as thou last interpreted to me, I will do all that thou desirest, and get thee brought out of this dungeon.

12 And the baker, seeing that Joseph had accurately interpreted the butler's dream, also approached, and related the whole of his dream to Joseph.

13 And he said unto him, In my dream I saw and behold three white baskets upon my head, and I looked, and behold there were in the upper-most basket all manner of baked meats for Pharaoh, and behold the birds were eating them from off my head.

14 And Joseph said unto him, The three baskets which thou didst see are three days, yet within three days Pharaoh will take off thy head, and hang thee upon a tree, and the birds will eat thy flesh from off thee, as thou sawest in thy dream.

15 In those days the queen was about to be delivered, and upon that day she bare a son unto the king of Egypt, and they proclaimed that the king had gotten his first born son and all the people of Egypt together with the officers and servants of Pharaoh rejoiced greatly.

16 And upon the third day of his birth Pharaoh made a feast for his officers and servants, for the hosts of the land of Zoar and of the land of Egypt.

17 And all the people of Egypt and the servants of Pharaoh came to eat and drink with the king at the feast of his son, and to rejoice at the king's rejoicing.

18 And all the officers of the king and his servants were rejoicing at that time for eight days at the feast, and they made merry with all sorts of musical instruments, with timbrels and with dances in the king's house for eight days.

19 And the butler, to whom Joseph had interpreted his dream, forgot Joseph, and he did not mention him to the king as he had promised, for this thing was from the Lord in order to punish Joseph because he had trusted in man.

20 And Joseph remained after this in the prison house two years, until he had completed twelve years.

[See the price we have to pay, when we trust in man!]

The chosen have been given a lot of power in their mouths, mind, and heart.

The chosen, being under a great anointing, you don't need to, and you can't afford to, let anybody know what you can do, and who you are.

Superheroes usually keep their identity secret, to protect not only themselves, it's also to protect those that they love.

People also would like to look at the chosen, just because of their abilities as they ohh ahh at their abilities, without knowing their story has been a roller coaster of up's and down's!

JASHER 71:1-4

1 And when Moses was eighteen years old, he desired to see his father and mother and he went to them to Goshen, and when Moses had come near Goshen, he came to the place where the children of Israel were engaged in work, and he observed their burdens, and he saw an Egyptian smiting one of his Hebrew brethren.

2 And when the man who was beaten saw Moses he ran to him for help, for the man Moses was greatly respected in the house of Pharaoh, and he said to him, My lord attend to me, this Egyptian came to my house in the night, bound me, and came to my wife in my presence, and now he seeks to take my life away.

3 And when Moses heard this wicked thing, his anger was kindled against the Egyptian, and he turned this way and the other, and when he saw there was no man there he smote the Egyptian and hid him in the sand, and delivered the Hebrew from the hand of him that smote him.

4 And the Hebrew went to his house, and Moses returned to his home, and went forth and came back to the king's house.

[MOSES AT 18 YEARS OLD, GOES BACK TO THE KING'S HOUSE, AS WE CAN SEE HE WAS RAISED FOR 18 YEARS AS A ROYAL EGYPTIAN]

JASHER 73:1-3

In the fifty-fifth year of the reign of Pharaoh king of Egypt, that is in the hundred and fifty-seventh year of the Israelites going down into Egypt, reigned Moses in Cush.
2 Moses was twenty-seven years old when he began to reign over Cush, and forty years did he reign.
3 And the Lord granted Moses favor and grace in the eyes of all the children of Cush, and the children of Cush loved him exceedingly, so Moses was favored by the Lord and by men.
[Moses at 27 years old, is a ruler in Cush, and ruled for 40 years]

JASHER 76:1-23

1 And Moses the son of Amram was still king in the land of Cush in those days, and he prospered in his kingdom, and he conducted the government of the children of Cush in justice, in righteousness, and integrity.

2 And all the children of Cush loved Moses all the days that he reigned over them, and all the inhabitants of the land of Cush were greatly afraid of him.

3 And in the fortieth year of the reign of Moses over Cush, Moses was sitting on the royal throne whilst Adoniah the queen was before him, and all the nobles were sitting around him.

4 And Adoniah the queen said before the king and the princes, What is this thing which you, the children of Cush, have done for this long time?

5 Surely you know that for forty years that this man has reigned over Cush he has not approached me, nor has he served the gods of the children of Cush.

6 Now therefore hear, O ye children of Cush, and let this man no more reign over you as he is not of our flesh.

7 Behold Menacrus my son is grown up, let him reign over you, for it is better for you to serve the son of your lord, than to serve a stranger, slave of the king of Egypt.

8 And all the people and nobles of the children of Cush heard the words which Adoniah the queen had spoken in their ears.

9 And all the people were preparing until the evening, and in the morning they rose up early and made Menacrus, son of Kikianus, king over them.

10 And all the children of Cush were afraid to stretch forth their hand against Moses, for the Lord was with Moses, and the children of Cush remembered the oath which they swore unto Moses, therefore they did no harm to him.

11 But the children of Cush gave many presents to Moses, and sent him from them with great honor.

12 So Moses went forth from the land of Cush, and went home and ceased to reign over Cush, and Moses was sixty-six years old when he went out of the land of Cush, for the thing was from the Lord, for the period had arrived which he had appointed in the days of old, to bring forth Israel from the affliction of the children of Ham.

13 So Moses went to Midian, for he was afraid to return to Egypt on account of Pharaoh, and he went and sat at a well of water in Midian.

14 And the seven daughters of Reuel the Midianite went out to feed their father's flock.

15 And they came to the well and drew water to water their father's flock.

16 So the shepherds of Midian came and drove them away, and Moses rose up and helped them and watered the flock.

17 And they came home to their father Reuel, and told him what Moses did for them.

18 And they said, An Egyptian man has delivered us from the hands of the shepherds, he drew up water for us and watered the flock.

19 And Reuel said to his daughters, And where is he? wherefore have you left the man?

20 And Reuel sent for him and fetched him and brought him home, and he ate bread with him.

21 And Moses related to Reuel that he had fled from Egypt and that he reigned forty years over Cush, and that they afterward had taken the government from him, and had sent him away in peace with honor and with presents.

22 And when Reuel had heard the words of Moses, Reuel said within himself, I will put this man into the prison house, whereby I shall conciliate the children of Cush, for he has fled from them.

23 And they took and put him into the prison house, and Moses was in prison ten years, and whilst Moses was in the prison house, Zipporah the daughter of Reuel took pity over him, and supported him with bread and water all the time.

[Moses goes from a young ruler raised in Pharoah's house in Egypt, to a ruler in Cush, and now he is doing 10 years in prison! The life of a chosen vessel is filled with up's and down's for a reason! The chosen must be tested, and prepared for their next assignments!]

JASHER 77:26-51

26 And Moses the son of Amram was still confined in the dungeon in those days, in the house of Reuel the Midianite, and Zipporah the daughter of Reuel did support him with food secretly day by day.

27 And Moses was confined in the dungeon in the house of Reuel for ten years.

28 And at the end of ten years which was the first year of the reign of Pharaoh over Egypt, in the place of his father,

29 Zipporah said to her father Reuel, No person inquires or seeks after the Hebrew man, whom thou didst bind in prison now ten years.

30 Now therefore, if it seem good in thy sight, let us send and see whether he is living or dead, but her father knew not that she had supported him.

31 And Reuel her father answered and said to her, Has ever such a thing happened that a man should be shut up in a prison without food for ten years, and that he should live?

32 And Zipporah answered her father, saying, Surely thou hast heard that the God of the Hebrews is great and awful, and does wonders for them at all times.

33 He it was who delivered Abraham from Ur of the Chaldeans, and Isaac from the sword of his father, and Jacob from the angel of the Lord who wrestled with him at the ford of Jabbuk.

34 Also with this man has he done many things, he delivered him from the river in Egypt and from the sword of Pharaoh, and from the children of Cush, so also can he deliver him from famine and make him live.

35 And the thing seemed good in the sight of Reuel, and he did according to the word of his daughter, and sent to the dungeon to ascertain what became of Moses.

36 And he saw, and behold the man Moses was living in the dungeon, standing upon his feet, praising and praying to the God of his ancestors.

37 And Reuel commanded Moses to be brought out of the dungeon, so they shaved him and he changed his prison garments and ate bread.

38 And afterward Moses went into the garden of Reuel which was behind the house, and he there prayed to the Lord his God, who had done mighty wonders for him.

39 And it was that whilst he prayed he looked opposite to him, and behold a sapphire stick was placed in the ground, which was planted in the midst of the garden.

40 And he approached the stick and he looked, and behold the name of the Lord God of hosts was engraved thereon, written and developed upon the stick.

41 And he read it and stretched forth his hand and he plucked it like a forest tree from the thicket, and the stick was in his hand.

42 And this is the stick with which all the works of our God were performed, after he had created heaven and earth, and all the host of them, seas, rivers and all their fishes.

43 And when God had driven Adam from the garden of Eden, he took the stick in his hand and went and tilled the ground from which he was taken.

44 And the stick came down to Noah and was given to Shem and his descendants, until it came into the hand of Abraham the Hebrew.

45 And when Abraham had given all he had to his son Isaac, he also gave to him this stick.

46 And when Jacob had fled to Padan-aram, he took it into his hand, and when he returned to his father he had not left it behind him.

47 Also when he went down to Egypt he took it into his hand and gave it to Joseph, one portion above his brethren, for Jacob had taken it by force from his brother Esau.

48 And after the death of Joseph, the nobles of Egypt came into the house of Joseph, and the stick came into the hand of Reuel the Midianite, and when he went out of Egypt, he took it in his hand and planted it in his garden.

49 And all the mighty men of the Kinites tried to pluck it when they endeavored to get Zipporah his daughter, but they were unsuccessful.

50 So that stick remained planted in the garden of Reuel, until he came who had a right to it and took it.

51 And when Reuel saw the stick in the hand of Moses, he wondered at it, and he gave him his daughter Zipporah for a wife.

[Moses never would have found the stick {staff} if he had not did 10 years in his future father-in-law's dungeon! Moses never would have been blessed with a good woman if he had not did 10 years in the dungeon! If you notice He was praising and worshipping while in the dungeon, he was not complaining about his condition!]

JASHER 78:7-10

7 In those days Moses, the son of Amram, in Midian, took Zipporah, the daughter of Reuel the Midianite, for a wife.

8 And Zipporah walked in the ways of the daughters of Jacob, she was nothing short of the righteousness of Sarah, Rebecca, Rachel and Leah.

9 And Zipporah conceived and bare a son and he called his name Gershom, for he said, I was a stranger in a foreign land; but he circumcised not his foreskin, at the command of Reuel his father-in-law.

10 And she conceived again and bare a son, but circumcised his foreskin, and called his name Eliezer, for Moses said, Because the God of my fathers was my help, and delivered me from the sword of Pharaoh.

JASHER 79:1-12

And in those days Moses was feeding the flock of Reuel the Midianite his father-in-law, beyond the wilderness of Sin, and the stick which he took from his father-in-law was in his hand.

2 And it came to pass one day that a kid of goats strayed from the flock, and Moses pursued it and it came to the mountain of God to Horeb.

3 And when he came to Horeb, the Lord appeared there unto him in the bush, and he found the bush burning with fire, but the fire had no power over the bush to consume it.

4 And Moses was greatly astonished at this sight, wherefore the bush was not consumed, and he approached to see this mighty thing, and the Lord called unto Moses out of the fire and commanded him to go down to Egypt, to Pharaoh king of Egypt, to send the children of Israel from his service.

5 And the Lord said unto Moses, Go, return to Egypt, for all those men who sought thy life are dead, and thou shalt speak unto Pharaoh to send forth the children of Israel from his land.

6 And the Lord showed him to do signs and wonders in Egypt before the eyes of Pharaoh and the eyes of his subjects, in order that they might believe that the Lord had sent him.

7 And Moses hearkened to all that the Lord had commanded him, and he returned to his father-in-law and told him the thing, and Reuel said to him, Go in peace.

8 And Moses rose up to go to Egypt, and he took his wife and sons with him, and he was at an inn in the road, and an angel of God came down, and sought an occasion against him.

9 And he wished to kill him on account of his first born son, because he had not circumcised him, and had transgressed the covenant which the Lord had made with Abraham.

10 For Moses had hearkened to the words of his father-in-law which he had spoken to him, not to circumcise his first born son, therefore he circumcised him not.

11 And Zipporah saw the angel of the Lord seeking an occasion against Moses, and she knew that this thing was owing to his not having circumcised her son Gershom.

12 And Zipporah hastened and took of the sharp rock stones that were there, and she circumcised her son, and delivered her husband and her son from the hand of the angel of the Lord.

[Now we see Moses feeding a flock, and almost killed due to not being obedient to what he was already supposed to do! The chosen live very challenging lives, however if and when they remain faithful, so many others are blessed as a result!]

STAY FAITHFUL CHOSEN ONES, YES I'M TALKING TO YOU!

YOU! YOU ARE CHOSEN THAT'S WHY YOU NEVER FIT IN!
YOU! YOU ARE CHOSEN AND THAT'S WHY YOU ARE FAR FROM NORMAL!
YOU! YOU ARE CHOSEN, SO THINGS NEVER HAVE WENT AS YOU PLANNED!
YOU! YOU ARE CHOSEN, AND ONLY A FEW UNDERSTAND YOU!
YOU! YOU ARE CHOSEN, AND THAT'S WHY YOU ARE OFTEN ISOLATED!
YOU! YOU ARE CHOSEN, SO YOU SEE WHAT OTHERS DON'T SEE!
YOU! YOU ARE CHOSEN , SO YOU HEAR WHAT OTHERS DON'T HEAR!
YOU! YOU ARE CHOSEN, AND YOU STRUGGLE IN RELATIONSHIPS!
YOU! YOU ARE CHOSEN, SO YOU CAN'T HELP HAVING A GOOD HEART!
STAY STRONG MY CHOSEN BROTHER
STAY STRONG MY CHOSEN SISTER
REMEMBER CHOSEN ONE'S, THAT EVIL, WILL LIE ON YOU, SPREAD RUMORS ABOUT YOU, PLACE BLAME ON YOU WHEN, IT'S REALLY THEM, AND DRAG YOUR NAME THROUGH THE MUD, AFTER THEY THROW MUD PIES AT YOU!
IT'S NOT EASY; HOWEVER OUR EXAMPLE BEFORE US, ENDURED IT WAY, WAY, WAY WORSE, SO WE MUST PARTAKE, JUST NOT ON THE LEVEL THAT HE HAD TO ENDURE!

MATTHEW 10:25

25 It is enough for the disciple that he be as his master, and the servant as his lord. If they have called the master of the house Beelzebub, how much more shall they call them of his household?

ALWAYS REMEMBER CHOSEN ONE'S THAT WE GROW AND LEARN FROM THE MANY AFFLICTIONS THAT WE FACE, AND ALWAYS EVENTUALLY ARE DELIVERED FROM!

PSALM 119:71

71 It is good for me that I have been afflicted; that I might learn thy statutes.

LAST BUT, SURELY NOT LEAST CHOSEN ONES WE HAVE TO DO THE CREATOR'S WILL AND WE HAVE TO OBEY HIS LAWS, OR ELSE FULFILLING OUR PURPOSE WAS IN VAIN! DON'T FALL FOR THE LIE THAT THE CHOSEN ARE EXEMPT FROM KEEPING THE LAW! MEN AND WOMEN IN THE BIBLE THAT DID NOT HEED TO THE CREATOR'S LAW WERE PUNISHED, AND ETERNAL PUNISHMENT IS FOR THE DECEIVED!

MATTHEW 7:21-23

21 Not every one that saith unto me, Lord, Lord, shall enter into the kingdom of heaven; but he that doeth the will of my Father which is in heaven.

22 Many will say to me in that day, Lord, Lord, have we not prophesied in thy name? and in thy name have cast out devils? and in thy name done many wonderful works?

23 And then will I profess unto them, I never knew you: depart from me, ye that work iniquity.

✓ BELIEVE IN YOUR CREATOR
✓ BELIEVE IN YOUR PURPOSE
✓ BELIEVE IN YOURSELF
✓ BELIEVE THAT YOUR DREAMS WILL COME TRUE, MINE !
- DR. MARTIN ALAN BRYANT
- CEO - AGED NOT

[FOR BACK COVER]
- ✓ Ever felt chosen for something, but felt almost frozen in place?
- ✓ Ever felt presently content, but felt the future holds more for you?
- ✓ Ever never quite fit in with your family, and friends for no reason?
- ✓ Ever had or felt abandonment issues in relationships?
- ✓ Ever felt compelled to do right, when you could do wrong?
- ✓ Ever felt like you can see, or hear what others can't for no reason?
- ✓ Ever felt like you are from someplace else and are feeling displaced?

I know how you feel friend, and if you don't feel this things, maybe your siblings, friends, or children feel any of the above things. You are not alone, and what you feel, or they feel is for a reason, and I'm purposed to bring clarity to your struggle, and therefore your healing and deliverance!
It is truly an honor to be blessed with a great purpose on your life, however; it's not; however it can feel like a curse, while you are in preparation to fulfill your pre-destined purpose in life!
I'm living proof of what occurs, when you trust the process, and where the pain in the process is taking you and how it is developing you!
I could never help anyone if I quit!
Quitters never win, and a winner never Quits!
- Dr. Martin Alan Bryant – H.E.A.L.E.R.

-

PHOTO GALLERY:

LATE IN THE Y/O OF 2023
[BY THE WAY, I HAVE NEVER JUICED, NOR WILL I, I'M A HARDWORKER, NOT A
CHEATER IN ANY SENSE OF THE WORD! DRUG **FREE** IS **ME!**]

I PUT A LOT OF WORK INTO MY QUADS (THIGH MUSCLES) WHILE GOING
THROUGH, AND LOOK AT HOW MUCH STRENGTH IS PRODUCED IN STRUGGLE!

LATE IN THE Y/O 2023

UPPER BODY STRENGTH PRODUCED AS A RESULT OF STRUGGLE! MY DAUGHTER 24 YEARS YOUNG AT THE TIME, SAID YOU COULD TELL BY THE LOOK IN MY EYES THAT I WAS UNDER IMMENSE PRESSURE AT THIS TIME! SHE WAS RIGHT!

LATE IN THE Y/O 2023

MY WAIST LINE AND BELT SIZE HAD TRIMMED WAY DOWN ONCE THIS PICTURE WAS TAKEN! I FELT BETTER ABOUT MYSELF, AND AT THIS TIME, THERE WAS NO MORE HAVING TO SUCK IN MY STOMACH TO BUTTON MY PANTS! NO MORE HAVING TO SHOP IN THE BIG AND TALL SECTION OF THE STORE FOR MEN EITHER!

MY 15 YEAR OLD SON AT THIS TIME, WITH HIS DAD, ON HIS DAD'S 54TH BIRTHDAY!

Y/O 2023

I LOVE ALL MY SON'S, MY 20 YEAR OLD SON IS AN ADULT AND AT THE TIME THIS BOOK WAS BEING PUBLISHED, WE HAD ..SOME CHALLENGES IN OUR RELATIONSHIP. I PRAY THAT WE ARE RECONCILED BY THE TIME THIS BOOK IS PUBLISHED, IN THE WILL OF THE HEAVENLY FATHER.

ME, WITH MY YOUNGEST SON, AND YOUNGEST DAUGHTER!
MY SON WAS 10 AND MY DAUGHTER WAS 8, AT THIS TIME! Y/O 2023

ME, WITH MY FIRST BORN, AND OLDEST DAUGHTER!

MY DAUGHTER WAS 24 YEARS YOUNG AT THIS TIME!

Y/O 2023

MY BELOVED MAMA ENJOYING HER 87TH BIRTHDAY

Y/0 2022

ME ENJOYING MYSELF AT A CARNIVAL WITH MY 2 YOUNGEST SEEDS! I'M SURE EVERYONE CAN SEE THAT I DON'T CARE ABOUT WHAT PEOPLE THINK ABOUT MY FLABOYANT SWAGGER! I RECEIVED COMPLIENTS [THAT I WAS NOT LOOKING FOR THANK YOU] ABOUT THIS OUTFIT, FROM MALES & FEMALES ALIKE.

Y/O 2023

PICTURE OF ME WITH A SHINER, AFTER BEING JUMPED ON BY A 6'5" 275 LB BOY.

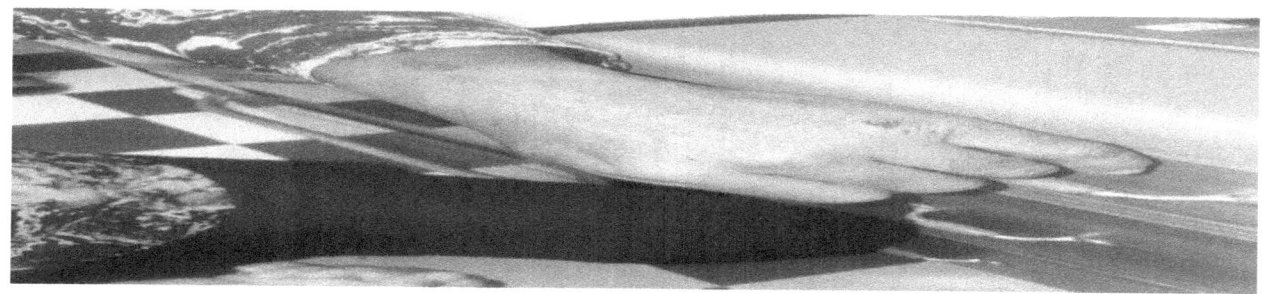

MORE DAMAGE DONE BY THE SAME 18 YEAR OLD, I WILL CALL BIG-D
I FORGAVE YOU BIG-D THE MOMENT AFTER THIS HAPPENED, THE CREATOR HAS DEALT WITH YOU ON THIS, BECAUSE YOU SHOULD NEVER TELL A 50 SOMETHING YEAR OLD MAN, THAT HAS ALLOWED YOU IN HIS HOUSE, TIME AND TIME AGAIN, THAT HE IS WEIRD, AND WORSE YET PUT UP YOUR HANDS, AND THEN TACKLE HIM, AND PUT BLOWS ON HIM, WHILE HE IS ON THE GROUND! AS I SAID I FORGAVE YOU, AND I'M AT FAULT BECAUSE I ALLOWED YOU TO CATCH ME SLIPPING..Y/O 2023

I HAD NOT WORKED OUT IN MONTHS, I HAD BEEN DIS-RESPECTED FOR MONTHS, I HAD NOT BEEN PRAYING AS I SHOULD FOR MONTHS, I HAD BEEN EMASCULATED FOR MONTHS AND I WAS OUT OF SHAPE, PORTLY, AND FULL OF WINE FOR MONTHS! IN PHYSICAL, MENTAL, & SPIRITUAL SHAPE, YOU WOULD NOT HAVE STOOD A CHANCE, I DON'T CARE HOW BIG YOU ARE! LESSON LEARNED, NONE [NOT BOLO, OR DEBO] WILL NEVER, EVER CATCH ME SLIPPING AGAIN!!!!!!!!!!!!!!!!!!!!!!!!!!!!! -
PERIOD

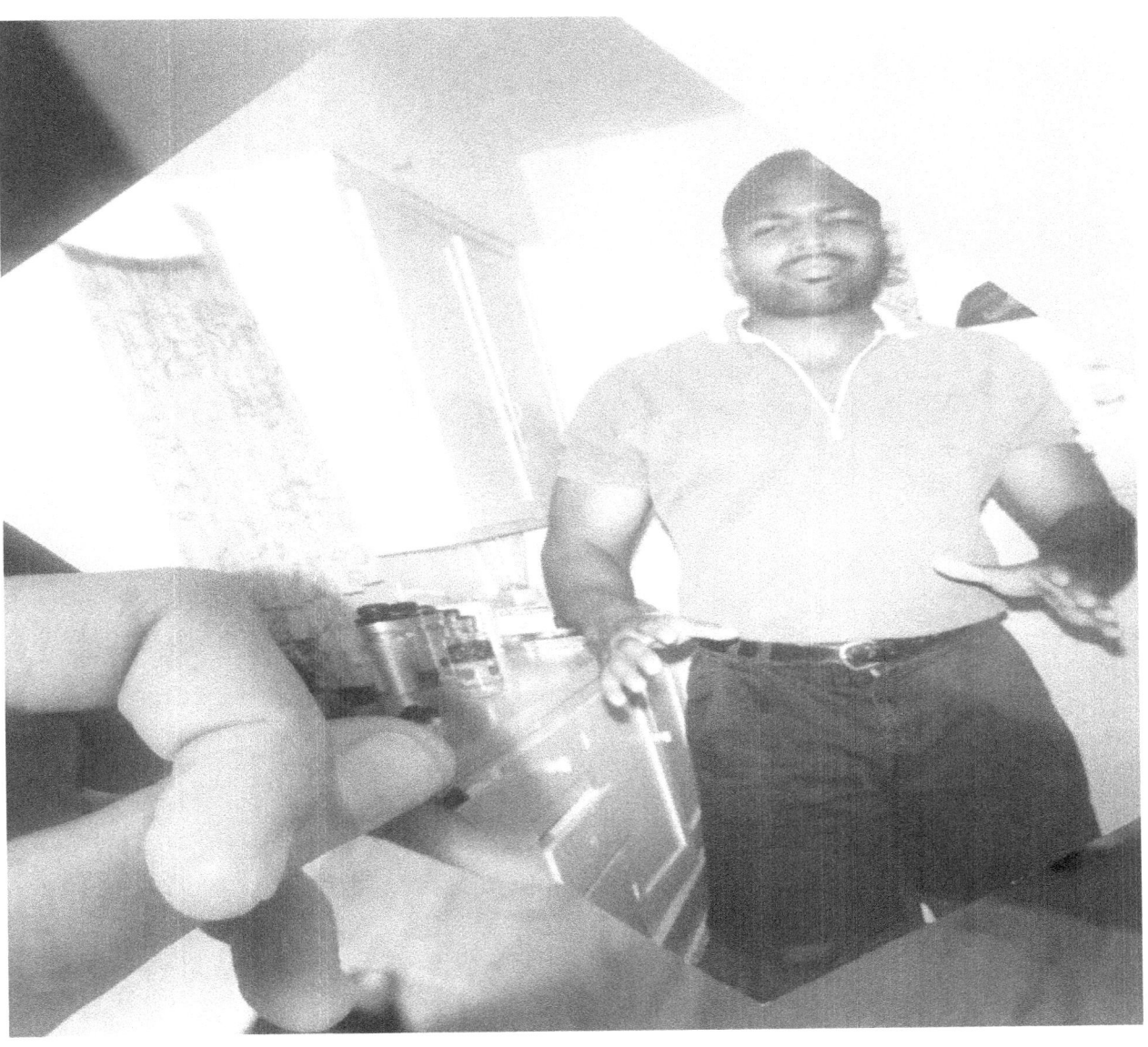

A PICTURE OF ME IN THE 90'S IN MY B.M. [BEFORE MESSIAH] DAYS, THINKING THAT I WAS RICO SUAVE!

Y/O 1998

I'M SO GREATFUL THAT THOSE DAYS ARE OVER, AND THEY ARE ONLY REMEMBERED FOR THE SAKE OF A TESTIMONY OF ME BEING DELIVERED BY THE POWER OF,

THE MOST HIGH

THANK YOU, ♥ *THAT I'M CHOSEN & UNFROZEN.*